poetrywivenhoe

*p*oetrywivenhoe

a collection of new poetry

selected by

Joan Taylor, Pam Job,
Peter Kennedy and Mike Harwood

Wivenbooks 2008

Wivenbooks 2008

Cover illustration:
"Orange Lifeboat" by James Dodds
ISBN: 978-0-9557313-2-7
www.wivenhoebooks.co.uk

CONTENTS

FOREWORD

by Dean Parkin

Poetry anthologies are mystery tours always worth going on, so I'm delighted to have been asked to provide a foreword to this book – a selection of vital poems from The Wivenhoe Poetry Prize, alongside those contributed by members of the society.

My highlights so far? Startling first lines like, '*Lying ear to armpit...*', the crackle and love of language evident in '*limp damp flowers, the ink-bled grief*' or the dazzling image of a trumpet that '*sprays its brassy notes, flaying the air, / rocking the ears of the deaf, / rinsing their hair with gold*'. You'll find poems that also tell stirring stories – the powerful pull of the past found in a photo in an old newspaper and the brilliantly envisaged, shocking poem addressed to a 'half grown child' who was hanged in Colchester.

*poetry*wivenhoe is one of those all too rare reading venues that combines an ideal location with an appreciative, attentive and enthusiastic audience. People that not only relish listening to poems but, on the evidence of this publication, are also dedicated and skilled poets.

Launched in February 2007, *poetry*wivenhoe's aim was to bring quality poetry events to Wivenhoe – they certainly have done that and can now add a quality publication to their list of credits too.

Introduction

by Joan Taylor, Pam Job,
Peter Kennedy and Mike Harwood

It indeed has been a remarkable mystery tour for the four of us who judged the inaugural Wivenhoe Poetry Prize Competition 2008, and selected from the submissions the poems for this book. The competition was sponsored by both *poetry*wivenhoe and The Wivenhoe Bookshop, whose proprietor Ginny Waters has been a great supporter of *poetry*wivenhoe events from the outset, and publishes this book under the imprint of Wivenbooks. We are extremely grateful to Ginny for everything she has done.

This book is not just a compilation from competition entries, however, but is also envisaged as a contribution to the nation's new poetry from people of a vibrant community and its surroundings. Wivenhoe, situated on the Colne Estuary not far from Colchester, has always been an unconventional little town, with a long history of remarkable sea-folk, fishers, ship-builders, smugglers, entrepreneurs and free-thinkers. Since the founding of Essex University in the 1960s, it has absorbed into its midst a variety of newcomers, including many students, academics and commuters to London, who congregate in the numerous pubs and bolster a variety of societies. It has for many decades had a thriving artistic, literary and musical community. Wivenhoe is known as being socially mixed, eclectic and friendly.

Launched in 2007, *poetry*wivenhoe was designed to bring high quality poetry events to Wivenhoe. Every month there have been visiting poets, with supporting local poets, who read to an audience of between thirty and seventy people. The meetings thus far have featured Matt Harvey, Martin Newell, Pauline Stainer, Derek Adams, Myra Schneider, Dean Parkin, Katherine Pierpoint, Matthew Sweeney, Robert Cole, Dave Charleston, Kathleen Jamie, Katrina Porteous, Kevin

Crossley-Holland, Alison McVety, Jude Simpson, Andre Mangeot, Andrew Frolish and Christine Webb, and there is an equally exciting programme lined up for the future. One feature of the meetings is the open mic session, providing an opportunity for anyone to stand up and read one or two of their own poems. The idea for this competition came as a result of us seeing how much good poetry was being shared.

The *poetrywivenhoe* organising team are poets too: Chris Tanner, Pam Job, Joan Taylor, Peter Kennedy, Mike Harwood, Adrian May and Philip Terry. We have included some of our own poetry in this collection so that it becomes a representation of the creative energy of *poetry*wivenhoe as a whole.

Many thanks to all the poets who have submitted their work for this collection. Out of interest, the prize-winners we chose – after much deliberation – were as follows: first place: Kate Lammin, *Shutters*; second place: Judith Wolton, *Jazz in a Town Park*; third place: Melanie Wright, *After Deciding Not to Make Love Because We're Too Tired*; Patricia Crittenden Bloom, *The Lamb in the Library*; Roger Caldwell, *Upstream, Downstream*; Tony Tackling, *Wivenhoe Park*; Peter Johnson, *Bru na Boinne*; Rex Hughes, *Invigilation*.

POEMS

06.00

Orion strides across the morning sky,
The blood-dark blue of nearly dawn, frost cold.
Across the marsh the water, wading-high,
Spreads silently, the flood tide three hours old.
A cow calls mournfully, in darkness sounds
Afloat, far out above the low sea wall.
Her voice is old and lone beyond the bounds
Of fence and herd. Soft breathing's rise and fall
Displaces nothing in the stillness, makes
No imprint on the air. The night grows thin,
All colour lacking, while Orion takes
His skylight leave. The peach-skinned dawn slips in
Through open ice-rimmed panes to touch the face
Of each, still locked in sleep and love's embrace.

Jane Hughes

AFTER DECIDING NOT TO MAKE LOVE BECAUSE WE'RE TOO TIRED

Lying ear to armpit, calm
muffled beating like a womb

smooth, smooth we breathe together
suspended eye in stormy weather.

The hairs around your aureole
wicked, wild, Welsh-browed, curl –

points of unreason in your body's
cultured logic. Remember heady

days when sex dripped from our skin
like an oversoaked sponge, when every sin

seemed an invitation? Gone,
drained in two-minute contractions

four-hourly feeds and eight
a.m. school runs (running late).

Dried, our terrain was strange, cruel
faults in arid clarity revealed.

We beat out ploughshares into blades
and reaped a hurricane of words.

Now twelve years of sharp edges
have all sandpapered down to this:

what we are, we are to keep.
I feel you soften into sleep.

Melanie Wright

AFTER THE CARNIVAL

I found it today,
proof of the evil of cities.

It was standing by the roller-doored kiosk
of the Edgware Road subway.
Various others walked past,
busyness moving them on.

But he stood still,
an old man and his puppet.

He in greys and browns,
his puppet in carnival colours.
Both heads hung low,
limbs of wood, eyes of glaze.

Urine stench seeped,
from everywhere and nowhere.

Others walked through it,
over it, above it.
But it had swallowed the old man,
consumed him, defeated him.

The city had pissed all over him.

Kirsten Broomhall

ALWAYS THE FLOOD

The fireman's pumping out the water.

It's always the flood,
though they said it was all going to end
with fire next time,
nuking us with fantastic, unnatural heat,
some heavy lightening
civilisation cooked in its own oven.

But after all it's always the inundation,
it's what you need and what you're made of;
engulfed by being neglectful, out of balance.

It's elements and essences, not achievements;
Fire we play with: Water we are.

It's always after us, the deluge,
And what it means,
what it meant for Noah and Gilgamesh
and the Kraken waking,
is that you've made too much noise
and now you're on your own;

sinking, still after the impossible
arc of a rainbow.

And the fire brings the flood.
And the earth brings the flood.
And the air brings the flood.
And the flood brings the Flood.

Adrian May

AM I COMMUNICATING?

'To add to that war against pain, to add to the expanding
army of the NHS we are harnessing resources – public,
private and voluntary – in more staff, more surgeons,
more treatment centres.'
(John Reid: Labour Party Conference 2003)

On April 17 2008
I left for the hospital shortly before mid-day
in our Mini Metro.

There were ten of us in the waiting room.
One flipped Hello magazine,
another put down a tattered Country Life.
None of us spoke a word.

We were saying hello to a whole new era:
A first wave of independent sector treatment centres;
A second wave of private finance initiatives;
A third wave of elite foundation trusts.
I carried inside me this backlog of spine ache
and for a moment I felt the discomfort swell sweetly,
in the war against pain.

I shall never forget that long afternoon wait
and the consultant's few words
as he requested me to strip to the waist.
I fully understood the necessity, the question
and welcomed his prodding knowledge.
But after four minutes – I'd been promised fifteen,

his glance stretched over my shoulder
to a clock on the wall.
'Am I keeping you?' I asked.
'Yes,' he said, 'I must go to a meeting,
staff development targets
with outside consultants
on how to communicate
better with clients.'

He left my pain
isolated
in the empty office,
surrounded by patient records.

I wrote my request for another appointment
on headed Trust paper,
placed it in the box,
a Walls ice cream tub, stubby with messages
on the closed reception desk.

Mike Harwood

ANGLES

One tower dwarfs another
(though the sun fades it to orange-grey);
two crows diverge at right angles
(and the third flies straight across the sky);
and the light through the curtains splays concentric circles
of mathematical precision.
So wait for nightfall.

The crinkling of a book's spine into vertebrae is random
but regular: each distance is measurable, and
though the water was spilled, its
carelessness is quantifiable: each drop has
volume; each breath is caught and weighed and
categorised.
So wait for the night.

With all the fleeting thoughts and small
pains, the dragging breaths and rhythms
of the day: wait for the dark,
where the sharp angles
break down and distances blur into blue
unmeasurability.
Sit on the quiet edge between sleep
and waking: the one drowning and the other
dry,
and watch the world
through the wavering
waters.

Tam Blaxter

ANNIVERSARY

Where else would she be?
Sitting staunchly upright
in beige knitted gloves,
pilled but still cosy after years
of making do and mend.

The coat is quality enough,
a bargain prized, a bit of a find;
its label black, stitched with gold,
reassuringly declares
no trace of polyester.

Downy white wisps escape
here and there from underneath
the silly pixie hood he gave her
as a joke when once they tackled
Box Hill in the snow.

Today the slopes, through
January rain, are indistinct.
Never mind. She perches
on plastic-wrapped supplements
for weekend entertainment.

Occasionally she turns, and with
a crumpled tissue from her pocket,
wipes away encroaching drops.
The brass plate smiles back at her
like a personal sun.

Sally Bowles

AN AWAKENING

Not always a winner, I've known success
Now and then, small gains earning modest praise
Enough to help me bear the weighty press
Of plodding, leaden, work-dull days.
There's never been glory, admiration
From cheering crowds braying their acclaim,
No heroics deserving of decoration.
No honours board ever held my name.
But now exuberance rules! I dance, bound,
Cartwheel, fight to control heartfelt laughter!
I'm king of the heap, ruler of all around;
A winner now! And for ever after!
    And the reason for my transformation?
    We've met and kissed at St Pancras Station.

Denis Ahern

BREAKFAST

A plate
A knife
A tiny army of brown skinned soldiers.
Each one bearing its name across a barrel chest,
Beneath the Doctor's scrawl,
'Twice daily with food.'
She seems almost proud of these little warriors,
Which guard her place
At the breakfast table.
A glass of water,
A jolt of the neck,
She swallows.

I see her clumsily powdered nose,
And sniff the ancient smell,
Which is my Grandma.
I watch her shaky hand
As she pours herself a cup of tea.
A dash of milk,
Tea from the chrome monument
Which marks the difference.
Into the slim-waisted cup
She purses her tight lips
And sips from the delicate porcelain,
Decorated with floral transfers.
Her little finger
Sticks out daintily – she hopes.

At the head of the table

My father wraps his farmer's hand

Around a stoneware mug.

The only decoration,

A scribed ear of wheat.

We eat

In a silence which will not nourish us.

Alison Kent

BRU NA BOINNE

Those who creep here first
carve the ground as their stones.
The sluggish water laps
their crops as rough boats scrape

its hinterland. They build
huts with split planks wedged in
trenches, dig pits in the dark,
hunker down by the hearth.

Eyes stalk their palisade.
Men drink the June waters
that will make a troubled
seer of Fionn Mac Cumhaill.

The great mound rises where
bones of sheep and cattle mix
with wheat grains in the earth.
Scrapers, blades and flakes are

swept from the soft soil on
the flood-plain of the Boyne.
Leavings litter the ground:
pigs' snouts, sherds of pot,

lip-turned to show their craft,
and leaf-shaped arrow-heads.
Their dead hide deep beneath
the plundered earth and stone.

Peter Johnson

THE BUS TO UZÈS

Admire the Roman engineers who built
   The Pont du Gard.
Like us they could accommodate their guilt:
   'We're who we are.'
Each of us finds the meanings that we seek.
   As Time marches,
The sun casts shade in la rue de la République
   Under the arches;

Shadows of medieval towers, the famed
   Tour Fenestrelle.
The poor bloody legionnaires cannot be blamed
   They tasted hell.
Shadows of Castle, and Duke, and all his men
   In the Bermonde Tower;
Renaissance splendour of St Etienne;
   Symbols of power.

I want to turn my back on Le Portalet
   And all it stands for,
Rulers and ruled, lords and the servants they
   Clapped their hands for;
Both victims of historic forces – pray
   For their liberation.
Sadness tames my anger at the way
   They messed up creation.

The longer I live the less I think I know.
    For far too long
Men who thought they knew have had a go
    And got it wrong.
I don't any longer want to change the world –
    It's me I fear.
I only trust in love. I wish I were curled
    Up with you here.

Love, let us trust our hearts and this stirring love
    Now the chips are down;
But then, I wonder if your friends will approve,
    If I'll fit in this town.
Preferring *boules* to running bulls, I feel absurd.
    Do I need
To admit I haven't read a single word
    By André Gide?

Strolling hand in hand through the market in
    La Place aux Herbes
I hear you hum, 'I've got you under my skin.'
    (The thought disturbs.)
Waking, I find I've drained the sauvignon;
    Now I've no excuses
Not to take the train to Avignon
    Then the bus to Uzès.

Tom Fenton

CAERNARFON CASTLE

We pay and enter an amphitheatre
Of green grass, and thick, high walls.
Walls inside walls hide spirals of stairs.

'Here! Here! I want to go in here!'
He's imperious, demanding, and I love him.
Exhilarated, I rush to be pulled into the dark.

Unsteadily in his bright flashy wellies,
he climbs, I follow, on steps worn by
soldiers, kings, servants, tourists.

A shallow step. I stumble. My heart beats as
my head enacts the tumble of us spinning
in the dark, towards the dank stone floor.

I snap, 'Be careful. Go slow! Watch Out!'
I am dizzy and sick, impatient and anxious.
I sound like another mother, not me, not me.

Where did I go? The girl who would climb
a steep, jagged cliff? The woman who
explored the world, alone and unafraid?

Later, on a wet park bench, I smile and clap
as he presents for me a fabulous battle
of bravery and strength. It is his turn now.

Petra McQueen

CARRYING SUNFLOWERS HOME

Squalls rip across the place
Scud, churn up clouded mirrors, the scalp of muddied grass
Darken, even, the dinginess, the trampled gum
Snatch at the tuneless fiddler, lurid in McDonald's glare

Into this tarnished greyness she lurches
Hugs the sunlit talisman, living ecstatic yellow,

Gives thanks, guiltily, that what was spilled there yesterday
Violently, inside the ring of limp damp flowers, the ink-bled grief
Was another woman's, yet another woman's.

Kate Lammin

CAT'S EARS

We frustrated you with our nests of secrets.
We took everything you threw at us,
soaking up spears of gauzy rain-
spikes blunted on our gravelly beds.
Sudden blisters of light seared us
for a moment until we licked them up
with casual sepal stretches.
We waved back at the black gales
rushing down from Moniack Mhor.
We took it all, silently shoring up
our labyrinths, spiralled forests of gold and ochre
in half globe cups.

One still night (you'd long gone)
we lay prostrate under the stars,
an army of new constellations pricking the fields.
We lay long-limbed till dawn.
Under the blare of the sun
we were threaded with pleasure.
In our own time
We gave ourselves up.

Chris Tanner

THE COURAGE TO BE

When a problem arises, be flexible.
The bathroom on the attic floor has an open skylight.
I cannot shift the iron catch.
I wash myself with the morning chill fingering my skin.
Outside is a chimney pot where a jackdaw sits every morning.
It ruffles its feathers and gives an experimental squawk before
it flies off into the day.

Clowning is all about relationships, making connections.
I am a human – the man holding me is my guardian angel.
My eyes are shut.
He encircles me with his arms.
He helps me move.
I find lost flexibility in my body, the warmth of touch, physical
recognition.

The first rule of clowning is to say 'yes' – even if you don't want to.
Possibilities, complexities, difficulties – these are what the clown
works with.
A sequinned purple headband, a rich black cloak with gold
embroidery, high-heeled brown cowboy boots – and always
the red nose.
I slip in and out of levels of reality.

Stay with the issue, walk around it, consider it.
We tell the tale of Rumpelstiltskin.
'I'm Gertrude,' Rob introduces himself to the audience.
'He's always Gertrude on Fridays,' I say.
I have to turn two plastic bottles into gold.
Desperate, I beat them on the floor.
If I don't succeed I die.

Get inside the experience. Look at us! Show us what you're feeling.
I look up at a light –
It becomes a star.
I gaze at it in wonder.
I stand there, looking at the star,
Which is a light,
Which is a star.

Caroline Phillips

DALIBRUGH

The wheelhouses of Cladh Hallan,
sunk so lately under deep sand,

lurk where the grass path swerves.
A desiccated girl was dug from one.

I see her lost and fractured
under the cool green turf,

hair tendrilled around a skull
filled with sand, softly packed,

snug then among those buried stones
since hauled to raise the graveyard wall.

The driftwood of the great ocean,
heaved out of the weltering froth,

is sawn and shaped to house the dead
in the machair's burial ground.

Lichen sprouts from the headstones
like mad green eyebrows.

Waders jet from the grey strand
and hurtle in a tight pointillist shimmer

where clotted waves slap on the rocks
and smear the surface, thick with kelp.

When I slip, your cool hand tightens
and you laugh as my heart beats.

Further out, through ruptured clouds,
light leaks onto a reef of water.

Peter Johnson

DANTE: INFERNO I

Halfway through a bad trip
I found myself in this stinking car park,
Underground, miles from Amarillo.

Students in thongs stood there,
Eating junk food from skips,
       flagmen spewing e's,

Their breath of fetid
Myrrh and rat's bane,
     doners

And condemned chicken shin
     rose like
          distemper.

Then I retched on rising ground;
Rabbits without ears, faces eaten away
        by myxomatosis

Crawled towards a bleak lake
     to drink
        of leucotomy.

The stink would revive a
     sparrow, spreadeagled on
     a lectern.

It so horrified my heart
    I shat

        botox.

Here, by the toxic water,
    lay a spotted trout, its glow
    lighting paths for the VC.

And nigh the bins a giant rat,
Seediness oozing from her Flemish pores,
Pushed me backwards, bit by bit

Into Square 5,
        where the wind gnaws
          and sunshine is spent.

By the cashpoint
    a bum asked for a light,
      hoarse from long silence, beaming.
When I saw him gyrate,
His teeth all wasted,

              natch,

His eyes
    long dead
    through speed and booze,

I cried out
        'Take pity,
Whatever you are, man or ghost!'

'Not man, though formerly a man,'
        he says, 'I hale from Providence,
                Rhode Island, a Korean vet.

'Once I was a poet, I wrote
        of bean spasms,
        was anthologised in *Fuck You.*'

'You're never Berrigan, that spring
Where all the river of style freezes?'
I ask, awe all over my facials.

'I'm an American
        Primitive,' he says,
'I make up each verse as it comes,

By putting things
        where they
    have to go.'

'O glory of every poet, have a light,
May my Zippo benefit me now,
And all my stripping of your *Sonnets.*

'You see this hairy she-rat
               that stalks me like a pimp:
Get her   off my back,

               for every vein and pulse
Throughout my frame she hath
                         made quake.'

'You must needs another way pursue,'
He says, winking while I shade my pin,
'If you wouldst 'scape this beast.

Come, she lets none past her,
Save the VC. If she breathes on you,
                    you're teaching nights.'

'This way, freshman, come,
If I'm not far wrong we can find
A bar, and talk it over with Ed and Tom.'

Philip Terry

DAWN AT LION POINT

Now is the time when day
sits silently
waiting.

Gulls stand still
on wet stones, shining –
resting their necks in hunched wings.

Tides hold back their waves
deep in the crab's hole.
Wind holds its breath in salty lungs
and dares not move the marram,
nor shift the glittering sand
spread out in long curves.

Sky is shelled in nacre,
oyster-still and cirrus high –
waiting.

The fisherman's boat
leans into the arc of dark rocks;
its black and ragged flags
bunched like an old bouquet,
hanging limp in its stern –
waiting.

Look across at the Odeon curve
of the thirties Sunspot Café,
catching the first rays,
warming its sluttish heart,
as it waits for the day to begin.

Judith Wolton

DISORDERED LANGUAGE

Around the table we sit, our annual assembly
to gather our words for judgement.
Forms filled in, duplicated, full of words.
Our guide takes up a sheet, talks of targets,
some fallen short, one overshot,
of growing confidence and mastery of the bow.

The flow of speech blurs the picture
of my bewildered son.

The tale is taken up by the woman
who speaks like a prophetess, reading the past and future alike
of this child of incomprehension, anxiety translated
into concrete example,
literal interpretation.

I begin to recognise his face,
vulnerable, trusting, uncertain,
the growing figure of approaching manhood,
long strides, joke-recalling, retort-making,
whose world is adrift, depths to be crossed,
no underlying continent.
Make no assumptions:
meaning is a gift.

Gloria Brooke

DREAM

I dreamt of you
steering a ship
through a narrow channel.
A huge ocean
lay at the end.
I held onto the wet railing
as the ship lifted and plunged
in the vertical waves.
Sometime later you showed me
the short videos
you had made.
I didn't know you had this skill.

I dreamt of you married
to another woman.

I tried to sleep one afternoon,
but all I got
was the beating of my heart.

Eliza Kentridge

DRYSTONE

Confident in their geometry
they hack up from the valley bottoms
with a colonial determination:
the reduction of wilderness
into chequered packets.
Still higher and we marvel
at the man who stacked up
limestone on limestone
in crazy tessellations.

Beyond here they career from
the buffeting of sheep.
West winds traduce their path.
No one planned
for the sly threads of lichen
the furring up of blue green mosses,
the gentle tugging to earth,
a final scattering of stones.
And now, beneath the skylarks,
the black peatlands,
keeping a silent communion.

Chris Tanner

EUROSTAR

On the train back from Brussels
On the train back from my family
Back to my family
Without enough chocolates.

Wondering what the past meant
And what all the words spoken mean,
And who we are,
The brothers and sisters,
Parents, nieces, nephews,
Friends, new faces –
The chef-patron watching from the kitchen
His wife weaving quietly between tables
In the hush of the words spoken –

Broken by the bang of the taxi door,
And the slow traffic
And running for Coach 17
Before time stands still
And waits for no man
And marches on,
The luggage safely stowed,
The city rolling backwards

And the memory of recent feasting:
Wine, artichokes and the pastry regretfully uneaten on the plate.
The regretful pastry,
And the purposeful bottles,
And the speeches full of love
Reaching out, all of us,
To touch someone wonderful.

Past the apple fields of Kent
And the electricity sub-station,
Horses in blankets,
Fields blaring yellow under a dark sky,

And I think of them,
All of my loves in their different places;
Staring at their plates.
Playing with their rings.

I think of the one in a green dress
And the one who pours a salve on our wounds,
The one in the white shirt,
The beauty whose eyes fill with anxiety.
And the one in his grey suit
Whose wings enfold us all.
My reflected hands twist a tissue.
His wings enfold us all.

Eliza Kentridge

EVENING ....

The estuary silt sucks in its gums
Tiny, plucking sounds, shifting
Myriads of unseen creatures
Their mud casts embellished, transformed
By a suddenly-sinking sun
Into the encrusted silver brocade
(displayed in Brick Lane shops)
Across which carries
The sharp pitch of seagull cries
Curlews' gentle gurgling, waders
Kicking up pricks of sunlight
And a sky still summer.

I watch your plane rise silently, (such weight!)
Beyond the whispering reeds whose
Leaves all point one way,
Fly up into blue, leave only
A trace of teased-out cloud trail
Disintegrating slowly. Insubstantial.
While you hurtle far and away
Until the red desert claims you.

Kate Lammin

THE FACE AT THE WINDOW

His small face pressed against the pane,
he stares out on an empty street,
in his imagination fills the view
with circus animals, with acrobats,
ladies in tights, a lone giraffe
– whatever's alien to an avenue.

Then in a stifling schoolroom as he sits,
scowling, at his desk, one in a line
of other scowling schoolboys too,
he waits for the Martians to invade
– the Sixth Form seems a life-time off –
but no cataclysm is yet due.

Then a university degree, a job,
and he's visiting his mother's house:
she says 'That girl's no good for you.'
He's filled with adolescent rage again.
No wonder that he needed to escape,
and yet escape-routes seemed so few.

Then babies, mortgages, more uphill paths,
commuter trains, and bills to pay.
He's so long standing in the queue
he forgets what he was waiting for.
What life, he wonders, would remain
were there no waiting left to do?
The face is at the window always.

Patience is the virtue needed,
asking that the world be made anew,
so that the elephants at last might come,
clowns, acrobats, the girls in tights
in sultry triumph down the avenue.

Roger Caldwell

FAMILY BIBLE

This book with the pictures is given
to Ada Elizabeth Johnson
by her father and mother

This Bible, solid, dark, forbidding,
rough tape along one parted edge
and heavy metal clasps sunk deep
into the other, weighs heavy on my lap.

Passed to me so furtively, black
with the irony of its heritage,
freighted with the family dead,
when was it uncovered last?

David plays before the Ark
with a white-skinned coterie.
His preternatural fingers are
charmed by liver-spotted gauziness.

Then, a revelation. Lying
frail, a hedge-hidden flower,
the birth of a labourer's daughter;
witness the hand of John Hill, minister.

One night so soon they'll wake and find her
loosing her small soul out upon the tide.

Peter Johnson

FAYYUM

Now, let me get forensic with your face
and show my lust for every pretty part.
(It's what we do for love these days. No grace
or dalliance or true exchange of hearts.)
Hair first – I'll dive into those well-sprung curls,
so densely desert-black, so tightly right.
I'll limn your fine-arched brows; a lick of furl's
your well-positioned ear. A nose to bite
and then I'll slip my tongue between your lips.
That slight moustache gives beauty gravitas.
Your blazing eyes light fires in me and strip
me naked in your gaze. My soul's outclassed!

See, all's not lost while I can fantasise
about some long-dead athlete's sand-filled eyes.

Pam Job

GARETH IN ESKDALE

We sit at the scarred board in the inn
among the freckled fields of Eskdale,
waiting for you to scoot around
the corner in your red faded Nova.

A long hour beyond the snarl of the M6,
your face is a shock below the thatch of hair,
less young and awkward than before
but now, suddenly, thinned, tanned.

You are an outdoor man, bringing
the sky into the dark lounge.
You want to run up Hard Knott
and Wrynose before breakfast.

Later, we head for Crinkle Crags.
The mist moves away, sharpening the
scoured ravines of Langdale as we
climb into a freshening wind.

When we skirt the stump of the rigg
you fork off to scale Bad Step
while we soldier around the base
and haul up over the shattered ridge.

The land falls away, shelves down
to Great Moss, over to the crush of Scafell.
We hutch up the final climb to Bowfell,
its split flanks sloughed and shaled.

You launch ahead, with giant
swallowing strides, until I see
your hand, dark against the light,
reach to grasp the line of the ridge.

When we reach that collision of stone
you are perched on the high rock,
eyes out to Barrow and the coast,
alive to every fleeting cloud.

Peter Johnson

GOOD FRIDAY

Dawn burst across the sky in a stream
of blood and newness, spilling
over the curve of the Orwell Bridge –
and I kept talking of beginnings
as if they happened every day.

You were bunched up and silent,
conscious of every fibre and sinew
and consumed with the closeness
of the red flecks spotting the tiny waves
on the estuary beneath us.

We fizzed into the ward, dreams coming
in small explosions like matches,
and they closed the blinds on the light,
leaving it behind: forever sunrise.
And all the things that led us here –

we washed our hands of them,
with cool blue gel, alcoholic cleanser,
squirted into our palms, rubbed
between our fingers, scrubbed
until the old layers of skin fell away.

The arrival was sudden and I took
the baby with my clean hands,
blood filling the lines and whorls,
painting maps from which to read
our futures – rebirth through birth.

His skin deepened like a new bruise
while we waited for him to swallow,
to cry out protracted vowels, toppling
over the edge of our own breaths.
My eyes consumed his fragile lines

marking out the boundaries between
you and I. What might have been
inherited, and what might not;
what blood-borrowing could be seen,
and what was hidden in his genes?

Andrew Frolish

HASTINGS

Family groups huddled on the steep shingle beach,
Herring gulls, perched on cars and buildings, swooping down to screech
Over discarded chips.

Fractious, sullen children throwing tantrums, demanding treats,
Parents mumbling estuary English, smoking fags, sucking sweets,
Munching chips.

Tattered posters advertising a show starring Joe Pasquale,
Tinny muzak from amusement arcades burbling frantically,
Every other shop selling chips.

Tattooed arms, shaven heads, tee shirt covered obesity,
Mobile phone conversations shouted aggressively.
Everywhere the scent of stale chips.

I want to shout 'My dad was a milkman, he and Mum brought me
on holiday here,
Sat in deckchairs on the beach, took me on the pier,
Bought me chips.'

But I have been grammar schooled and universitied away
To another country, higher or lower I would not could not say,
And I am an alien, clutching my bag of chips.

Brian Ford

IN A SECOND HAND BOOKSHOP

Ah, this morning I was sweeping outside,
sweeping away the dead leaves and such,
for which I normally use a bag
– I sweep the dirt into a bag –
well, I'd neglected to bring one out with me,
so I left my neat pile of dirt and leaves to be scattered
by the wind –
yes, a bright morning,
but quite a breeze on her –
I passed a small car parked across the road
and noticed a woman at the wheel,
seeming to hunch forward rather sharpish,
and a lad in the passenger seat,
I wouldn't be surprised if it was her son,
resplendent in baseball cap,
sank into *his* seat, half-turning away,
which I thought peculiar –
(He drew out 'peculiar' into the mouthpiece)
– I thought maybe they were watching me.
Well, these days one can never be sure.
I left with a copy of Williams.

Tony Tackling

IN MEMORIAM

On my desk, a copy of *East Coker*.
Price: one shilling in 1941 –
Three months before my father's death.
The inscription, to my mother, says
'*Because she lives her own life.*'

I try to call up the woman of those words:
Strong, independent,
Young – with everything possible and a shining marriage.
One who inspired this gift of poetry.

'*In the beginning is my end.*'
My father drowned.
'Thirty-five officers and men blown up in a small boat,'
My mother said –
A lie – but part of living her own life.

The poem starts on page seven.
Further pages have been roughly cut.
They are stapled together unevenly.
The front cover is presentable.
The back cover had been burnt by fire.

Charred edges challenge the text.
Below the words, harsh and jagged
Silhouettes of destruction
Lie, one behind the other,
Discoloured by the smoke.

'*In the end is my beginning.*'
Later she gave the poem to me.
After her death
I read that '*to make an end is to make a beginning.*
The end is where we start from.'

Caroline Phillips

IN MOTION

In her dreams she moves and travels
but tonight first must clean
a cupboard of glass.

Inside,
sixteen crystal plates
piled like a dusty see-through high-rise,
strangely inhabited:
a layer of lice on each floor.

She begins to unstack,
they hike
over her wrists, countertop, the sink.

Sweating, she plucks and squashes, squashes and plucks.
The cat joins in,
gestures with flared nostril to the ones she's missed,
urges with his eyes to take the tissue to them.

Finally the last
is smashed,
and tweezered with fingernails
from between the hairs on her arm.
Almost too small to kill, to know it's dead.

The baby waits in the rucksack,
watching the cat.

She covers its small, bald head
with a gortex cap,
fastens it beneath the chin,
slips the straps over lean shoulders,

Closes the door behind them.

Faith Ressmeyer

INNOCENCE AT FUNERAL
(For PCE)

No one knows what to say to the bereaved woman
Who has lost her young son
The schoolboys huddle nervously
Their faces bowed. Their eyes averted from the scrutiny
Of what they might possess in thought or loss or feeling
As the weeping eyes of the dead boy's mother
Search each frightened boy in turn
Seeing in each one her son
Brother silent next to brother
The mourning party, reflecting quietly
In the half-lit room
A funereal conspiracy
Seems to have overtaken each boy
Sitting next to the silence of each boy
Each boy the dead boy's brother
A circle of humanity, together
But, strangely, how can it be so? Totally alone
One by one the boys leave the mother
To what memories and silences there can be
Silence now – Free from the call of her young son
Silence in the young boy's room.

Benjamin Gray

INVIGILATION

Quieter than a meadow full of cows
This room, where delicate hands,
Like ever-hungry sheep, graze on paper,
Steadily dropping loops and blots and lines.
Invisible, an intellectual load
Bows down athletic shoulders; tangled hair
Falls threadlessly; lips part only for yawn
Or sigh. The clock moves on.

Rex Hughes

IVY

At night, ivy clings to the brick of my mind;
thoughts vein up the wall, dig millipeded roots
in to keep a hard hold, climb with vim,
and I am awake, stuck with vital ponderings.
I can't clear them, sweep a clean slate of sleep.
This ivy of pains and purposes, mental wanderings
on what just happened, what might happen, keeps on
growing, lush and strong, in the stretched minutes,
hours, of moon-filled dark. Ivy sticks, firmer glued,
and sleep is covered over with creeping leaves,
shining trinities of worries that lead to other worries
with tendrils curling possibilities of what might be,
might not be, and if I did, and if I didn't, does she
like me, does he not, and dangers, believings,
weaving higher with each spine of fresh growth.
I turn and turn, tear away the ivy, rip it down,
smooth my hands over the clear surface of sleep
and pick off the pasted feet of this vicious vine,
pull it all away with a deep haul of breath
and concentration. I scrape it out.
A moment of peace.
But there again it holds, and grows once more
from scraps springing new roots and new leaves,
a vigorous vegetation of thoughts and thoughts.
I lie awake, moon-eyed, covered in ivy.

Joan Taylor

JAZZ IN A TOWN PARK

Observe the marks that music makes.
The piano stencils toe prints
on the surface of the pond.
See how the singing of a violin
draws vibrant lines
across the air.

And underneath a drum beat
scoops out hollows, flinging its notes
around and out to thud on walls,
smudging the pastel plaster
with purple umber, floating
echoes up to wash the sky.

The double bass sends curving brush-marks
rippling over the bandstand's canvas,
smearing its shades to a soft
magenta bruise.

A strident trumpet sprays
its brassy notes, flaying the air,
rocking the ears of the deaf,
rinsing their hair with gold.

Watch, as a melody etched in glass with
sharpened blades of lime-green jazz,
cuts its path through the listeners,
flying up and over their heads,
travelling the streets between high buildings,
painting its blue notes, edged with ochre,
high on the roofs and chimneys, then
releasing honey-bronze to drip in soft staccato,
soothing the acid wound of a minor key.

Grace notes flatten the dance to contemplation.

So the prints of sound are gently trodden down –
daubed violet in a sweet adagio,
touching the listeners' skin,
stroking their veins' linings,
making them quiver and weep.

You can feel them moving slowly,
tuning your muscles and bones,
testing them out, and
leaving their marks inside you.

Judith Wolton

JOHN CLARE VISITS LORD EXETER AT BURGHLEY HOUSE

He comes a day late
from waiting for the snow
to leave the Helpston furrows,
fearing his only shoes
would blot the shining floors.

The footman's sneer
leads him to upper reaches
of the house, meandering
through shoals of rooms
and sweeping corridors.

To close each door
springs sweat into his hands.
He hates his hard-nailed shoes,
that creak into the calm,
and fight the marbled floor.

The Marquess, dry and kind,
allows him half an hour
and fifteen pounds a year,
then points him to the hall
where the servants feed.

He stows the words away
but his eyes shy to the door.
He cannot stir a foot and
his tongue, thick in his mouth,
betrays his deference.

Loosed,
he stands within the lane.
He feels the words rush back,
ablaze with cries of birds and
a scythe's insistent swing.

As dark begins he walks
past ravaged ground, where
hired men are sledging posts into
beloved land and rooting
at the fibres of his mind.

Peter Johnson

THE LAMB IN THE LIBRARY

Open the book and these lines spring out:
'...eighteen women and a half-grown child
were taken from cells in Colchester's castle,
and hanged.'

Child! Untold is your story, of being disturbed
at the salt-pans, the herd strangely restive,
a newly-lamed calf at your side; how the drover
fussed with the air making signs of the cross,
swore you were hexing the land, named you
misshapen-get-of-the-devil, then hastened
to busy the world with his tale.

On Mistley quay, you crawled among spillage
begging for knuckles of coal to feed
your poor fire. Hungry, half mad,
you ached to be warm, to feel heat
in your belly instead of the swill
you'd cupped from the trough.

Scratching your way into dreams, your hoof
lap-cradled, the whaler's boy spinning his yarns
of sea-maids – with no feet at all – who beguiled
tall ships with a flick of their tails...
A laugh cracked your sleep and you came awake
wet with a longing to be tenderly held.

But the arms were violent, and the voices
of whales that swam in your skull, sank
to a moan when they hauled you ashore
mud clogging your throat, your thumbs
still tied to what passed for your feet.

The crowd crept away. Better, they muttered,
the Stour's cool kiss
than the Witch Finder's fevered embrace.

So then, as you crazily twisted in air
your bleating choked off by the rope's
fierce bite, only *then*
was your passing given scant note
and recorded onto the page.

Patricia Bloom

LEDA

I'm five miles high, unsure if what I can see
is the feathered edge of cloud or the littoral,
whether the droning is the engines or
the roar of air on wings, when I flick to
our new painting; Woman at the Window,
back view, naked, her hair-dusted shoulders
slightly hunched, light blushing her skin.
A curved floor tells me it's the old windmill
in Norwich. Her gaze at bright empty sky
is not an observer's cool perspective
but one responding to the song of space.
Hung as if she'd face the estuary,
she'll be at home with water and the swans —
woman and her bird transmuted into one.

Sally Festing

THE MAN IN FULL

I think you'd like him, brittle as he is
a man imagined out of balsa-wood
who when he's volunteering, works so hard
he bags three stars for his enthusiasm.

Names are nouns he *knows*, as soon as heard.
If you're his friend: you're *perfect*, you're *superb*.
That sound you're hearing's his heartfelt applause.

He's talkative at speed so garbles words.
His *toe-teckters* are boots with tips of steel.
His bicycle can take him forty-miles
from hereabouts to Brightlingsea and back –
St. Christopher will swerve him from harm's way.

To his best girl he makes platonic love.
They meet for basic suppers with red wine.
They'll watch an evening's worth of DVDs
then part, according to unwritten rules
insisting they must sleep and dream alone.

I think you'd like him. He does sensitive.
He wears extreme emotions on his sleeve.
He is a burster into sudden tears
on hearing havoc-news or curt remarks.
He takes offence as easy as dropped hats.
He is bewildered by complexity.

He hates the football stopping Emmerdale.
he hates the way his TV will not work.
As I'm his friend and he's innumerate
I am supporting him to write a cheque.
His trust in me is very beautiful.

I think he'd like your house of curled-up cats.
His phobia is one that sweats of dogs
of any breed their owners take on walks
to ruin his, across midsummer fields.

William Hampton

MOONSWIMMING

We arrive in the inky rain when the gasping sea
grips the sky and hangs on. The boat bucks and heaves
as we step into the waves holding our sodden packs
over our heads ridiculously. Black water slips and turns
between the mangrove roots, twisted fingers concealing
secret eddies and currents and all the detritus gathered
in the fists of the silent trees. Ghosts of plastic bags snag
and guard the beach like an army of jelly fish.
Quietly, like strangers, we tread between roots,
fearing hidden dangers, fearing the secrets
that might trip us, break us.

Safety, and the morning light soars unexpectedly –
last night's storm gathered up and flung out to sea
(only for the tide to bring it back later
and hide it among the mangroves).
The daylight exposes the sharks' teeth among the stones
on the beach and blisters our skin silently.
I find myself in the dark places: the cave of bats along the shore;
the secret lagoon fallen deep into the limestone pinnacle
like an empty eye socket.

The day ends, suddenly lifting the moon,
spilling over the black and silent sea.
We swim alone, cooled and naked and glistening,
entwined like seaweed, twisting together, muscular eels
between the mangrove roots, making more secrets.

Andrew Frolish

NIGHT, SUMMER

Gulls knowing nothing
wrong
   glide slowly down, so
slow, with eyes black
   to that horizon,
in fact, they're out of
place to minds
stricken by
   departing suns,
fading redness,
fire as if rain,
as if static,
on the water,
   which is significant,
if not urgent,
when someplace is waiting,
somewhere you must be,
   but barred,
as they settle against tide,

and make no sound
nor move.

Tony Tackling

NIL BY MOUTH

'Nil by mouth,' it said.
Yet he smiled a warm welcome
and kissed me from his bed.

His mouth shaped his thoughts
into words to tell me of
all aspects of his heart.

As I left he pursed
his lips, as if to say 'no' –
then softly wolf-whistled.

Ann Clarke

NOWHERE IS SAFE:
MISSOURI AFTER 9/11

Nowhere is beyond reach now,
not even Hannibal, Missouri, home
of the annual frog-jumping competition,
of the Hannibal Pirates' Friday night
high school football game.
But things had changed already
when topless dancing came
to Old Milt's Tavern.

Nowhere is safe now, not even Hannibal.
Could Tom Sawyer's Cave
become a fall-out shelter?
Why is there a guard in place
outside the federal courthouse?
Why are the locks and dams
across the Mississippi
now put out of bounds?

It's impossible to be too careful.
Nowhere's beyond the reach of Satan.
Anxious Southern Baptist preachers meet
in Hannibal's Mark Twain Dinette
and over ham, eggs, hash-browns ask
why God is punishing America.
Is it for allowing Mormonism?
Should abortion be outlawed?
There's a cluttering of nervous knives and forks.

But business must go on as usual.
The Big River Discount Store stays open,
the next Big Truck Show must take place,
though the cops – preparing for a threat
against the Mark Twain Memorial Bridge –
eye with suspicion
a stray dog loping down
Hannibal's sunny half-deserted streets.

Roger Caldwell

OCTOBER NEST

This stillness has a name, it hangs beneath
the kitchen eaves caked and combed in silence.
Last spring it held a queen, jostled by armies
and vociferous young.

I knew such movement once!

A week and always gone, my bright-haired girl,
gone to join that bustling swarm
of other daughters, other sons,
two thousand miles away.

Into this empty house the silence flows
to claim its own, filling hallway, kitchen
TV nook. Her room. I listen
for remembered sounds as
echo-chambers brim
to clamorous quiet.

Patricia Bloom

ON THE WAY HOME

Streamers of blossom
cascade from the cherry tree.
The lawn is being snowed upon.
Elvis Costello on the radio sings
it's been a good year for the roses.
A blizzard of petals
fleets past the window.

You are on the way home
whirling down the country lanes
in front of the bawling rain.
I sit with an armful of hope.
You swirl in through the door
and out again
with your armful of promises.

Peter Kennedy

OUR CHERISHABLE CHILD

Our cherishable child is smooth and fat.
He's fed champagne and chocolate,
on holidays, apparently.
He mimes *I went by road and plane.*
The destinations sound bravura,
colour-rich exotic states –
the kind his family prefer.

Our cherishable child mimes lifting weights.
They're pygmy ones though still a strain,
But his gym instructress says:
no pain, no gain. For turning tired
he malcontents and head-down sulks
and burns two holes into the floor.

He waits on Friday afternoons –
to call me by my name as *friend*
with whom he'll play three frames of pool
of course to win and punch the air.
He is our cherishable boy-man-child.

William Hampton

OUT OF THE BLUE

We'd had a fight.
I'd left you at the airport stony-faced, gunned
the engine, driven south along the Interstate
heading for the beach.

Sand-flies salvoed into skin, but what
brought me to a halt were *butterflies*:
cloud after cloud of Monarchs drifting overhead,
those at rest emblazoning the rocks
or fallen helpless, to wet sand.
Tilting among the salty pulp of wings
a battalion of crabs.

The sweep of seasons and urgencies
of blood provoke nature's fierce
displays (beauty never was
her last resort). And now

she's at her tricks again, this time
in Regents Park. Snow drifts across
the summer beds – patterned tulips
lost beneath the white.
I draw the curtains close.

Behind this latest hotel door as
London's roar subsides, I pace from side
to side. Beneath my feet the carpet swirls
and heaves. I check the time; wait.
Wait now with seasoned readiness,
your unsettling return.

Patricia Bloom

PICTURE

You said, 'Look, Mum, it's the Simpsons' sky,'
light blue with white fluff gliding
and we walked off with Tara, white-furred body
wobbling down the farm road.
Our treads crunching on ballast, we looked
to great gold spools on the textile spread
of cut barley, to silver-braided river, ships.
We passed an artist building her acrylic landscape

in a frame, boxing it into four corners
and then walked in, like Mary Poppins, as she gazed.
For a moment we trod over her painted pathway,
the two of us and white dog mirroring the clouds.
There was a patch of cattle, like a palette
you could dab, and I said, 'Look, Em,
they're tan, and black and white, all together,'
But you were scared. 'Quick,' you said, and we

crunched on past flying flies and huge mouths
chewing cud, not noticing we were one short
till we had reached unbovined air.
Tara had stopped, not trusting wire and wood
against a herd stampeding, sensing small dogs
trampled. Calling, calling, we urged her,
yet the chasm of cows between us stayed.
At last, you strode back, fearless, put Tara on her

lead, and marched with her like Supergirl
pulling a child on a cord from quicksand,
as she arced far from the careless cows,
and then towards me, seeing the future wood.
You said, 'Mum, let's do some painting soon,'
but here I paint with words what brushes
do not do for me – the world of summer day,
my brave daughter, and a moment fit for creation.

Joan Taylor

POEM FOR DAD

Today
All the white petals fell from the rose
My beautiful rose.
And all that was left of the strong stem
Was an invisible spiral aspiring heaven bound,
Umbilical
Connecting the clay to beyond the stars.

Amber Giles

THE POETRY OF PARKING
(OR, THE PARKING OF POETRY)

There's nowhere to park your poems
Poetry City is full
from Shakespeare to Larkin
there's no room for parkin'
there are no spaces at all

From Caedmon to Heaney, each anthologised meany
is blocking the High Street you circle so keenly
and the Beats fill the one underground
the Romantics are up the high multi-storey
and the Pay-and-Display's full of Pound

Eliot's outside the bankers
there's Auden's butch Audi again
Ted Hughes' muddy old four-by-four
is blocking up Primitive Lane

Old JH Prynne, he won't let you in
to the tight, obscure space where he'll stay
some once tried virtual concrete parking
but they all got taken away

Each new poet's ego roars in the chorus
our genius must surely make spaces for us
If the Muse won't sing, we'll drive her, force her
in our dreams each poem's a brand new Porsche

Someone passes in a souped-up Sestina
by the myth-mobile of Yeats
and envies the parked their permanence
O, we would park with the greats
but that laurel crown's a wild notion
while we all just do the auto-Motion

We all know all the spaces are taken
yet more new poets drive round and round
they run out of fuel, get clamped, towed away
get fined, blocked-in, heavily bound
or they break all the rules and try stopping
anywhere and fly-park yellow lines
where poetry's forbidden 'at any time'
and incur just more break-downs and fines

Poetry City's a once pretty place
but now full of posturers, piles
posing, polluting, in flashier cars
on this doomed circuit, clocking up miles
till they crash like the dodgems of styles

They jostle and preen in each poet's machine
each one thinks they're the newest, the best
but each is a jerk
though their body of work
says its special, they're just like the rest

They're stuck in the old one-way system
they've not heard of the word poetasters
they're wasters and petrol-head versificators
all are just boy-girl poet-racers

They just want the status position
to be seen with all those in favour
published by Faber and Faber, and Faber
and Faber, and Faber and Faber

But there's nowhere to park your poems
rev it up all you like
it's not witty or pretty in Poetry City –
and that's why I'm riding this bike

Adrian May

QUINCES

This house is warm with eastern scent tonight,
steamy and strange exotic perfumes play,
teasing our senses, whetting our appetite.

The quince is hard, its core enamel white,
showing a perfect star when cut away,
this house is warm with eastern scent tonight.

Raw flesh is sour and grainy, tough to bite,
grey down on yellow skins is rubbed away,
teasing our senses, whetting our appetite.

Solon decreed this fruit a marriage rite,
each bride should eat one on her wedding day;
this house is warm with eastern scent tonight.

Symbol of fertility and sensual delight,
a cure to ease a glutton's gripes away;
teasing our senses, whetting our appetite.

Our quinces are preserved in jars sealed tight,
jellies, jams and pastes are stored away;
this house is warm with eastern scent tonight –
teasing our senses, whetting our appetite.

Judith Wolton

RENDEZVOUS WITH THE BLUE GREY MAN AT TATE MODERN

Ghost steps,
Ghost walking

The soft shoe shuffle of the Thames
A dangerous dancing partner;

He is as slick as paint
Polished as shellac,
His moves are the flick
Of a beetle's carapace.

A silent waltz,
A portentous polka,
A tenacious tango.

He invites you,
Waiting on the bridge,
One dance only,
Your twist to his rhythm.

The last waltz,
A seductive step,
A languorous weave
Of serpentine turns.

Until you beg for breath.

His sinuous arms and that
Familiar blue tattoo
Bind you

Expelling pure bubbles of joy.

Carole Webster

SCHOOL IN THE WOODS

'Today, we will be investigating:
The shapes of leaves and their
decomposition;
varieties of trees.'

'We will identify and name.'

The children look at
the life of bugs, for grossness
and, with climbing in mind,
check out trees.

'We will be sketching:
Leaves with opposite and alternate veins,
lobes and serrations;
birches and chestnut trees.'

The children draw
just leaves, yellow or brown,
and trees.

'Further remember:
No sitting
on the ground or on trees.'

'About eating:
Don't.
Do eat in your own time:
Berries or chestnuts
when they've fallen from the trees.'

'And:
Remember
to
walk
on
the
paths
in
single
file
till
we're
there.'

Trying to walk, the children run
and wonder about trees.

Marian de Voogt

SEA POEM

There are islands
lifting smooth or sharp, low
or towering, above the abrasive sea.
The air, here, is clear:
sharp and sweet
(though I can still taste the
taint of salt) and on the beaches I breathe
easily. But the heights call
with seagulls' scraping laughs
and I wander – alone, or with you –
up towards rain-channelled heights
concrete coloured,
iced with curling green like
a month-old birthday cake.

On the cliffs, breath grows thin as a balloon
stretched to transparency,
or wafer-sliced bread gone stale. From here
it seems a long way down; but the air bears weight like autumn ice
and I slip to the crust of the far-off sea
and break the surface.

Down here, vision is limited.
I can only see a few feet ahead –
beyond that all dissolves into a grainy cataract
obscuring nothing:
the nothing that stretches out around me
and which I cannot see.

This impenetrable water: like amniotic fluid

entering ears and nostrils

drips in the back of the throat like chilli

or vomit

stinging around delicate eyes' edges

and the grazed nailbed of my left index finger.

The cold forces thoughts inward, and the water pours in to fill their place.

It lies: a murky insulating layer inside my skull.

I do not stare into the obscured nothing

or think of the brash, physical pangs

of living

but retreat back and shrink

down to the size of the fish eggs floating

transparent

millimetres from my cornea.

Tides churn changing and

sometime I am washed up again,

bright and dry, unfazed on a white

hot beach. But mist seems to have fallen

and sometimes the cold creeps back up from the

waters' edge, and

I cannot remember which place this is,

and whether or not

to take a breath.

Tam Blaxter

SHENFIELD

The advertising board tells me to invest
and I should be grateful
it doesn't tell me to smoke,
though I want a cigarette,
but the platform's no-smoking.
I have nothing to invest.
One of those trains goes past,
a freight train,
with countless empty container spaces
and as I 'stand clear of the platform edge'
for the 'through-train approaching',
I play the game of wondering
whether I could jump and grab hold
and ride with the wind in my face
all the way to Norwich.
A schoolgirl sits cross-legged,
texting on a bench, dangling her shoe
and I watch. The train's delayed.
The announcer's voice has a thick prole to it.
The orange brick buildings on the platform
remind me of the buildings I saw last night
in American colour footage
of the liberation of a Nazi concentration camp in
Poland.
All that's missing is the soldier who looked fat
posing next to a pile of twig-like corpses.
The sky was green then too.
A rat scurries beneath the tracks,

in between an old bottle of Orange Tango
and a sole Nike trainer.
I walk into the small café on the platform
and get robbed for a double whiskey and ginger ale.
Soon I'll be back in Colchester.

Tony Tackling

THE SHOOTING PARTY

Aligned, we stand in distinct silence
Staring hard at flat grey cold
Damp seeping into beaters' bones
Pegged, we hold breaths waiting for birds to breach
Effortless above winter wrecked trees
The line swings on lone hen taking flight
With a flitter she has nothing more to teach
Other than how we can eliminate subtle life
With unnatural emphasis of heavy guns
What could withstand those odds ...

                                        Eight to one

Kirsten Molyneux

SHUTTERS

No longer black and white, this photo,
But ageing, a scrap of newsprint exerts
A powerful pull, exposes
Some undeveloped mystery.
Three women grouped, their backs
Betray an urgency.
Waitresses, crisp with starch, cake-frilled
Outside Lyons Tea House, framed
As they put up the shutters
In the deserted street.
One, more bold, half-flirts, turns,
Is seduced by our gaze,
Clutches another's arm, magnifies
The silence, the impending devastation.
 I can hear the air-raid siren and

Remember a mother of fine eyebrows,
Fox-head snapped round scarce shoulders,
Gloves, of course, and GI nylons,
Clopping hurriedly to meet
A man not my father
Whilst I, unknowing, complicit,
Perch high on a sticky stool,
Aim a long spoon at
A knickerbocker glory, as tall
As myself, but infinitely coloured,

Seductive, a child's guilty excitement,
An undeserved prize,
Blinded, not understanding how
Such splendour that stopped-up my mouth
Stole away my eyes in that Tea House,
Would seep slowly into a father's mind –
Leave a shadowy print of betrayal.

Now, on Remembrance Day
I pay for a scarlet poppy.

Kate Lammin

SKY DREAM

I nailed the linen sheet
on all four sides around the wooden structure
the long lath rectangle
that stood against the wall.
I nailed it thus, and thus.

Did you feel in your soul
the nails piercing the white sheet,
the folds straining towards
the corners, the linen belly
floating and ballooning, the whole
arrangement of a sudden seeming
as if it might lift itself up,
lift itself up and fly away
forever turning in the streaming
wind? White, billowing,
a floating, flying, rectangle
hurling itself up towards the blue
sky and forever ceasing to be.

Did you feel within your heart that you
yourself might be carried away, flying
with the white flying linen?

Peter Kennedy

SMART
(after Miroslav Holub)

Birds
 always instinctively know how to move and act,
 when to congregate, generating minim music
 on telegraph wires.

Project goal setters, however,
 lacking such instincts resort to motivational
 targeting, its effects illustrated by the following
 incidents.

A certain teacher
 was ordered 'to precisely tick boxes' after every lesson.
 Being a teacher he did so. When he was questioned for
 missing a tick he explained:

'I went by
 your absolutely SMART instructions, casting a completely accurate
 SPECIFIC tick, MEASURABLE tick, tick, ATTAINABLE tick, tick, tick,
 REALISTIC tick, TIME - TARGETS tick, tick, tick, tick.'

He knew
 that this method of management was absolutely useless.
 All that was left was to use his instincts, to cast off the tight
 lesson plan. He delivered a spontaneously inspirational
 session: insight; spirit; flair.
 Jack Par and Fran Fox came to life, for once;
 they said they would behave.

'Oh,' said the pedant,

    'this is missing the point. Consider,

    how can we judge the attainability of your performance

    if you don't follow our specific SMART goal programme?

    Your realistically set targets will lack time-bound

    motivational measurability.'

Birds

    Birds know when to gather to emigrate,

    how to pitch and plunge in flight.

    How not to glance another's wing, when massive turns

    form swirling clouds of dark clustered beauty.

Mike Harwood

THE SNAKE

He came again,
The snake,
Into my house this time,
I saw him lying
Slender on the stair,
And gazed at him
And he at me,
The two of us in disbelief
At what we saw.
At length my fingers lifted him,
His form adapted to my clumsy grip,
His yellow-bellied verdant body
Quickened its pulse,
And I carried him out through the house
To the edge of my territory.
I think of him now in his jungle of knotweed
And wonder at his coming
Into my house,
Resting upon my stair.
And I remember Lawrence
And feel honoured
As he was honoured
By the visit of a snake.

Angela Winn

SO LONG ...

I waited for you to die
so long,
in wards heavy with swollen-headed babies
and parents' faces jaundiced with grief.
You were a regular; nurses knew your name.
Undressing revealed a twisted body,
skin criss-crossed with shiny scars,
a clumsy mosaic,
a collage of a child.
I waited for you to die
not long now,
in a life light with empty pleasures,
and parents' faces smooth with pride.
I was a regular girl: I was what you were not.
Undressing revealed a strong straight spine
skin unscarred, long functioning limbs,
created by a master,
with the luck of the gods.

I waited for you to die
so long ago,
in heaviness, believing I'd criss-cross my skin,
and face my parents with double grief.
But life was regular; I was here and you were not,
except
undressing my son with his strong, straight spine,
skin unscarred, long functioning limbs,
you are in his blood,
alive with possibilities.

Petra McQueen

A SONNET FOR THE SHIPYARD

Alkanet, blackberry bramble and broom,
colt's foot, goosefoot, goosegrass and germander,
dogrose, daisy, jack-go-to-bed-at-noon,
lizards and newts and the local dittander,

buddleia, buttercup, poor man's brush,
cow parsley, cow parsnip, jack-by-the-hedge,
blackthorn and hawthorn, sharp-flowered rush,
goatsbeard and hawksbeard and salt meadow sedge,

herb bennet, herb robert, poppy, plantain,
pink campion, white campion, ragwort, restharrow,
crane's-bill and stork's-bill, thistle, fleabane,
kidney vetch, tufted vetch, toadflax and yarrow,

red clover, white clover and ribbed melilot,
all gone; the developers levelled the lot.

Elly Robinson

THE SONY BOYS

The Sony Boys are coming, dip your ensigns
Salute the techno-cultural advance.
Link GPS to laptop, wheel and engines,
We'll take you to the Channel Isles, or France,
Risk free. We have eliminated chance.
Establishing connection's not a battle.
Now see the British sailor's wit enhance
Kit from Japan, and software from Seattle.

The Sony Boys are coming: hide the booze.
We're surfing down our screens at seven knots.
Culturally, you've nothing left to lose.
The Sony Boys are calling all the shots.
The Yacht Club bores are knocking back their tots.
'Barmaid, another round!' The barmaid's gone.
She's gazing at a screen of moving dots,
Cyber-sailing the bays of Erewhon.

The Sony Boys are huddled down below
Hour upon hour. The Ship is sailing blind.
'We Sony Boys don't need to see – we *know*.
And what we don't, our search engine will find.
Old-fangled look-out? Leave that stuff behind.
Our screens are clear when what *you* see is fog.
Sailing, our laptops can control the wind.
It's just another entry in the log.'

The Cabin Boy looks up at stars and moon.

In laptop glow the Sony Boys are ghouls.

The Cabin Boy expects disaster soon

Not from the sea or rocks, but this ship of fools.

Decide, before our heritage unspools.

Rewind the history tape, reset the trip.

He disconnects the batteries; hides the tools;

Opens the seacocks; shouts, 'Abandon Ship!'

Tom Fenton

SPOON

Now that she lives
in the step-children's house
she chooses her spoon
with care when laying the table.

A cheap spoon, different from theirs,
brought from her home. It marks
her place at their table.
Somehow she thinks

the family won't notice
or remark on its presence –
its only a spoon at her place
on the table.

Judith Wolton

STEPHANIE FLANDERS

Whose financial reports demand exacting standards,
Bringing clarity to commerce's obfuscating melee?
None but elegant and articulate Stephanie Flanders.

When false flags are flown on untrustworthy lanyards
She exposes their duplicity for all to see
With financial reports demanding exacting standards.

The shady deal's done with bribes and backhanders;
Who sees through doors closed to you and to me?
None but elegant and articulate Stephanie Flanders.

When politician kow-tows and regulator panders
To tyrant and arms dealer all on the Q-T
Whose financial reports demand exacting standards?

Who cuts to the chase when the pack still meanders,
Her keen eye a-twinkle with inquisitive glee?
None but elegant and articulate Stephanie Flanders.

Who detects inside trading and sly money launderers?
Who's Miss Joan Hunter Dunn with an economics degree?
Whose financial reports demand exacting standards?
None but elegant and articulate Stephanie Flanders.

Denis Ahern

SUMMER LANGUAGE SCHOOL, ESSEX UNIVERSITY

'It has been suggested that architect Kenneth Capon's vision of the university campus was influenced by medieval Italian towns, particularly San Gimignano in Tuscany. Known as the 'medieval Manhattan', San Gimignano has a population today close to that of Essex University, and a number of compact, public squares dominated by several large towers. Unlike Essex, it is not made of concrete' (from Colchester, Capon and Concrete, by Graham Burton).

In summer, the place returns to its conceptual root:
San Gimignano delle belle torri, though these towers
rise in concrete from Constable's countryside, not
nestled on Tuscan hills. A strange conceit it is to map
brutal sixties breeze block to medieval marble, as if
such grift could graft Italian soul to Essex heartland.

I see them in the square, exchanging looks,
heat of teens so far from home, frustration free.
These lissome hips and latin eyes need
no shower to loosen wet desire. They bring
steam with them, rising from liquid syllables:
Silvia, vuoi venire nella mia stanza? Sei bellissima.

Such a change from term-time's angled Saxon elbows,
keeping touch at bay until the props of propriety melt
in pints of lager, finely balancing
pissed enough to and not too pissed to dance.
Christ, I was drunk convenient cloak for passion's shame,
careful choreography of want and fear.

It shouldn't be like that. I think, how sad
is winter's muffled English love, prematurely grey, afraid
to dance and laugh and be a holy fool. I wish
they'd come to summer school, unlubricated, creaking,
and soak up this sunstreaked open oily joy:
Silvia, vuoi venire nella mia stanza? Ti amo.

Melanie Wright

SWAN SONG

Snapshots taken thirty years apart
dulled your twice-worn gown to grey,
stripped corn-silk hair of shine, blurred shape.
Mindful of the tricks of light and age
the boneyard years have braced us
side by side.

As fledglings, framed by this church porch
we'd leaned above the lake, greeting
cob and pen at nest – mates for life.
We vowed to brave all distances
all weathers; vowed to be as true.

Today, unkempt and faithful as a hound,
the old church hunkers down among tall
grass, its welcome muted, tired.
We scan the lake, black opal
brushed with rain. Coots
and mallards agitate the reeds.

Wings, slapping first at water
then at darkening air, usher up
a cruciform of white rising
slowly from its mirrored self
a single swan, ghostly, mute.
Bereft.

No camera raised nor promise made this time,
no frame to hold oblivion at bay. The wine stays corked.
Wind spins across the buried bones to roustabout
in trees, pelts us slyly with petals. A few
catch in your hair.
Memory holds.

Patricia Bloom

SWIMMING LESSONS

Only a small hotel pool
a glasshouse with grey suburban Saturdays
swishing outside and leaking in.

There were too many elbows clamped to sides
fingers clacking at chins, skinny knees knocking
and too much noise.

Bob Ingolia wore a thin white strapless bathing cap
which meant he also wore a wig
or was just Italian.

He demonstrated the breaststroke
I squeezed for a view around jumping shoulder blades
saw only an upside down backstroke.

When it was my turn
tried to imitate.

Only years later did I learn to glide
and to float face down in
a jellyfish hush.

Faith Ressmeyer

TEN PERFECT TULIPS

Ten perfect tulips
have sprung from the tubs
a bloody foreground
a controlled explosion
a small army clustered
tall bright effervescent

lower reaches are protected
by sharp green scythes
they stand for days
without fainting
silently screaming to the sky

blood leaks upwards
to flush each petal
to blush each cheek
blooming soft in the gaze
of the purple velvet at their skirts

now a slight breath moves
fat trembling heads
cushioned on taut fuses
held under tension and
denying every word

when shadows fall
they will rise fiery
and illuminate the dusk

Roger Caldwell

THREAD OF LIFE

She peels her daily apple
without breaking once its skin.
The garland drops from her knife
and writes on the table
the same letter each time.
She looks out of the window
and sees the grass yellowing.
In the distance sounds
the constant rattle
from the shooting range:
soldiers practising for death.
She turns and finds
her reflection in a stillness:
the tranquil Penelope on the wall,
who hides and then doesn't
behind her cloth, coming
daily undone.

Marian de Voogt

THREE TREES, WINTERING

Sequestered, now swaddled
In bubblewrap
Three trees wait-out winter
Under glass.

A fig, leafless, bound to a stern grid
Defies such symmetry, pushes
Diagonals mischievously across,
Impatient, although just January,
For the show to begin,
For excess to swell up and
Litter the branches with
All the riches of summer
So the lover of figs
Becomes satiated.

Nearby, a calamondin, whose branches
Wave only westward, as if
A harsh sea breeze had worn away
Its youth, carved out a shape
Worthy of Willow Pattern
Where, amongst tender leaves
Proudly thrust up is the
First-ever fruit that crept
From the sweetest single flower
After a long dearth.

The last, a tree grown from an unknown seed,

By a lover, once dear,

Now bears only acrimony, whose spikes

Lacerate the silent hand

Forever trying to repair

A song that slipped away

Through careless fingers

Rustling, silkily past autumn

Into winter's ether.

Kate Lammin

TRYING TO FIND NEW WORDS

You come to me in dreams the sun still warm
in the hair of your arms.
Turning in our talk, slowly, I wait
feverish and thin behind my teeth.
You offer yourself in precise sips.
Parched, my tongue grows thick
with rage and longing.

Waking, fists pressed to belly
I want the weight of you,
the tenseness of muscle
bunching beneath my hands.

(A snarl of hills bite upward at the moon
 yellowed as an old apple and tumbling earthwards.)

Hungering, my lungs suck at the darkness
seeking your trace ... fresh-sour
as lemons, pungent as rough
warm steps of bread.

Hearing a tap against the pane,
I thought you had returned.
The great moth lay in the palm of my hand
silvering my fingers. Cecropia!
How it feels to have held you!
Pollened wings that beat down miles
to mate, crumbled at a touch.

Thoughts beat now among a thicket of words;
transfixed on the page they are as rigid as insects
under glass.

Nothing moves.

Patricia Bloom

UPSTREAM, DOWNSTREAM:
AFTER JEROME K. JEROME

Days on the river: upstart clerks
with handlebar moustaches, wearing
stripy blazers, and young socialists
in knickerbockers, earnest girls
reading classics in new Everyman editions.

Innocent times — those small secure Arcadias,
when playing the banjo was all the rage,
young couples spooning in the summerhouse,
and three spruce wasters out on a spree,
snaking their way upriver to Shepperton.

But no times were ever innocent
or ever will be. Mackintoshes,
unfurled umbrellas against driving rain
can't shroud what's floating on the river,
hair outspread, the dead face calm.

Though even after this the games go on,
if at first subdued, for fun's to be had
under the willows at Kempton Park
at five o'clock. New patterns on the water
as a boat turns this way, and then that.

Stories from long ago, of course,
and fashions change, but there will always be
someone rowing hard to Maidenhead
against the current, and for no good reason,
and an upturned boat that's floating, slow, downstream.

Roger Caldwell

WIVENHOE PARK

The child dances with a picture
on the field beside the lake,
jigging, her brother wanders up and
they both jig. Then they chase a duck
and their mother watches them.
They've nothing to worry about.
Whatever the picture is, it's been printed
on a side of A4, and I can only guess
from up in Rayleigh Tower
what the picture is of. I hope
it's a picture of Antonio Benedetto Carpano,
the inventor of vermouth, because
I'm drinking a fifth Manhattan,
but that's a long bet.
It's been a long day.
A gull flies again closely past the window
and the sun sets. Sophie says something
about making dinner, puts her book down
and leaves the room. The children stop chasing the duck
and begin jigging again. It's not
discovery that matters, it's the poem,
the memory, the cigar cutter,
and so I now find the point
and go clip on a Havana bought in town.
By Christ, I'm here, I am here.

Tony Tackling

THE ZEN OF HOUSEWORK

A clean house signifies a wasted life.
No chance. I sweep my bedroom with a glance
and slowly peel an apple with my knife.

I run my finger through the dust – it's rife.
Stardust, earth's chippings, my inheritance.
A clean house signifies a wasted life.

Cells, follicles, scales of mites,
all that's lived before can enhance.
I slowly peel an apple with my knife.

Each patina's a fecund slice of grief,
so many deaths are heaped to lie by chance.
A clean house signifies a wasted life.

'A duster gives lustre,' cries the housewife,
flicking sunlit motes. 'And there's good riddance!'
I slowly peel an apple with my knife.

My philosophy's to live, let die
and watch a beam of sunlight make dust dance.
A clean house signifies a wasted life.
I calmly peel an apple with my knife.

Pam Job

INDEX

Printed in the United Kingdom
by Lightning Source UK Ltd.
135149UK00001B/70-87/P